I0409663

Department of Defense Contractors in Afghanistan and Iraq: Background and Analysis

Moshe Schwartz
Specialist in Defense Acquisition

Joyprada Swain
Research Associate

May 13, 2011

Congressional Research Service

7-5700

www.crs.gov

R40764

Summary

The critical role contractors play in supporting military operations in Afghanistan and Iraq necessitates that the Department of Defense (DOD) effectively manage contractors during contingency operations. Lack of sufficient contract management can delay or even prevent troops from receiving needed support and can also result in wasteful spending. Some analysts believe that poor contract management has played a role in permitting abuses and crimes committed by certain contractors against local nationals, which may have undermined U.S. counterinsurgency efforts in Afghanistan and Iraq.

DOD relies extensively upon contractors to support overseas contingency operations. As of March 2011, DOD had more contractor personnel in Afghanistan and Iraq (155,000) than uniformed personnel (145,000). Contractors made up 52% of DOD's workforce in Afghanistan and Iraq. Since December 2009, the number of DOD contractors in Afghanistan has exceeded the number in Iraq.

According to DOD, in Afghanistan, as of March 2011, there were 90,339 DOD contractor personnel, compared to approximately 99,800 uniformed personnel. Contractors made up 48% of DOD's workforce in Afghanistan at that time. This compares to December 2008, when contractors represented 69% of DOD's workforce in Afghanistan. According to DOD data, the recent surge of uniformed personnel in Afghanistan and the increase in contract obligations did not result in a corresponding increase in contractor personnel.

DOD obligated approximately $11.8 billion on contracts performed primarily in the Afghanistan theater of operations (including surrounding countries) in FY2010, representing 15% of total DOD obligations for the area. From FY2005-FY2010, DOD obligated approximately $33.9 billion on contracts for the Afghanistan theater, representing 16% of total DOD obligations for the area.

According to DOD, in Iraq, as of March 2011, there were 64,253 DOD contractor personnel in Iraq compared to 45,660 uniformed personnel in-country. Contractors made up 58% of DOD's workforce in Iraq. Contractor and troop levels have decreased every quarter for the last nine quarters. DOD obligated approximately $15.4 billion on contracts in the Iraq theater in FY2010, representing 20% of total DOD obligations for the area. From FY2005-FY2010, DOD obligated approximately $112.1 billion on contracts for the Iraq theater of operations, representing 19% of total DOD obligations for the area.

A number of analysts have questioned the reliability of DOD's contractor data. DOD officials have acknowledged data shortcomings and have stated that they are working to improve the reliability and the type of data gathered. DOD is implementing a database to track and monitor contractor personnel during a contingency operation. DOD has also taken a number of steps to try to improve how it manages contractors in Afghanistan and Iraq, including efforts to centralize contracting support and management; implement regulatory and policy changes, train uniformed personnel on how to manage contractors; and increase the size of the acquisition workforce in theater. A number of these initiatives have been reflected in or were the result of legislation.

This report provides a detailed analysis of contractor personnel trends and contracting dollars obligated in U.S. Central Command (CENTCOM), Afghanistan, and Iraq.

Contents

Figures

Tables

Appendixes

Contacts

Background

The Department of Defense (DOD) has often relied upon contractors to support military operations. During the Revolutionary War, the Continental Army relied on contractors to provide such goods and services as transportation and engineering services, construction, clothing, and weapons.[1] Since then, advances in warfare and technology have expanded the functions and responsibilities of contractors in military operations.[2] After the Cold War, reliance on contractors further increased when DOD cut logistic and support personnel.[3] As a result of these cuts, DOD lost in-house capability and was forced to rely even further on contractor support.[4] Many analysts now believe that DOD is unable to successfully execute large missions without contractor support. These analysts point to recent contingency operations in Iraq, Afghanistan, and the Balkans—the three largest military operations of the past 15 years—where contractors have comprised approximately 50% of DOD's combined contractor and uniformed personnel workforce in country (see **Figure 1**).[5]

---

[1] Deborah C. Kidwell, "Public War, Private Fight? The United States and Private Military Companies," *Global War on Terrorism* Occasional Paper 12, Combat Studies Institute Press, Fort Leavenworth, Kansas, 2005, p. 9. See also James F. Nagle, *History of Government Contracting*, 2nd ed. (Washington, D.C.: The George Washington University Law School, 1999), pp. 16-19.

[2] Congressional Budget Office, *Contractors' Support of U.S. Operations in Iraq*, August 2008, p. 12.

[3] CRS Report R40057, *Training the Military to Manage Contractors During Expeditionary Operations: Overview and Options for Congress*, by Moshe Schwartz, p. 1.

[4] For example, in 2008 the Government Accountability Office (GAO) found that the Army had a contract for 11,000 linguists because DOD did not have the number of linguists needed. See U.S. Government Accountability Office, *DOD Needs to Address Contract Oversight and Quality Assurance Issues for Contracts Used to Support Contingency Operations*, GAO-08-1087, September 26, 2008, p. 6.

[5] For purposes of this report, DOD's workforce is defined as uniformed personnel and the contractor workforce. DOD civilian personnel are excluded from this count. According to DOD's *Joint Personnel Status Report*, as of September 8, 2009, the DOD civilian workforce in Iraq was 2,033 employees (less than 1.0% of the total force) and the DOD civilian workforce in Afghanistan was 1,706 employees (1.0% of the total force).

Figure 1. Contractor Personnel as Percentage of Workforce in Recent Operations

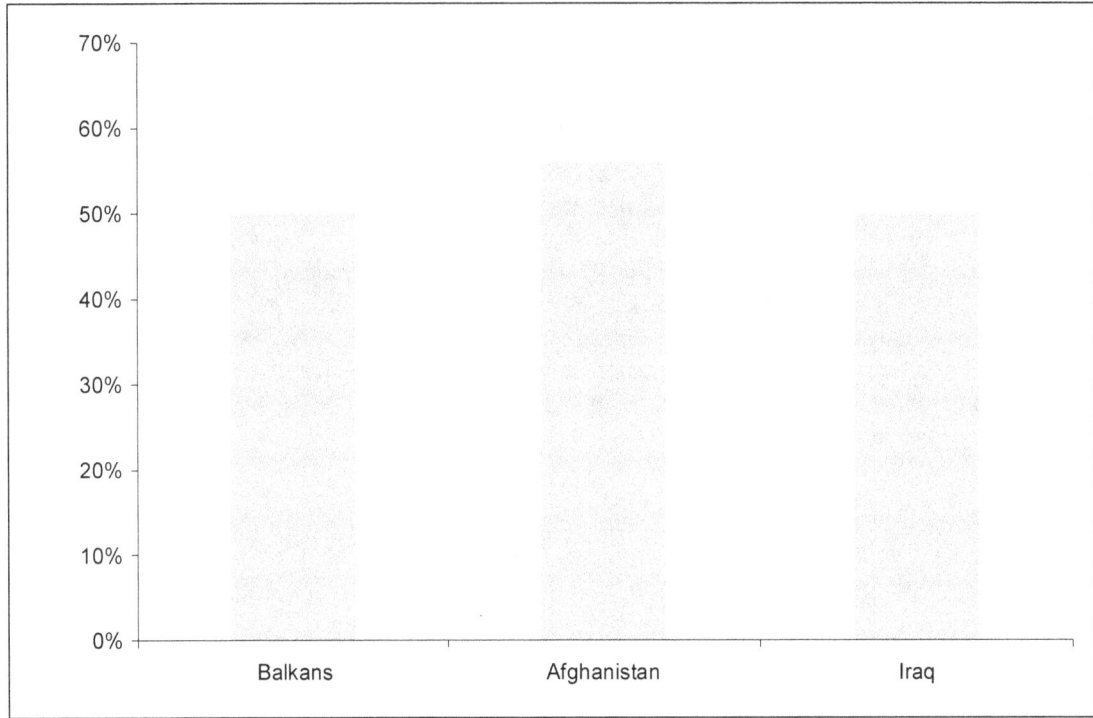

Source: Balkans: Congressional Budget Office. *Contractors' Support of U.S. Operations in Iraq.* August 2008. p. 13; Afghanistan and Iraq: CRS analysis of DOD data, calculated as an average for the period September 2007–March 2011.

Contractors are often seen as providing operational benefits to DOD. Using contractors to perform non-combat activities augments the total force and can free up uniformed personnel for combat missions. Since contractors can be hired faster than DOD can develop an internal capability, contractors can be quickly deployed to provide critical support capabilities when necessary. Contractors also provide expertise in specialized fields that DOD may not possess, such as linguistics. Using contractors can also save DOD money. Contractors can be hired when a particular need arises and be let go when their services are no longer needed. Hiring contractors only as needed can be cheaper in the long run than maintaining a permanent in-house capability. Using local nationals as contractors could also help develop the local economy and workforce, contributing to stability and counter-insurgency operations.

Managing Contractors During Contingency Operations

Lack of sufficient contract management can prevent troops from receiving needed support and lead to wasteful spending.[6] In addition, some analysts believe that lax contractor oversight may lead to contractor abuses, which can undermine U.S. counter-insurgency efforts.

---

[6] U.S. Government Accountability Office. *Stabilizing And Rebuilding Iraq: Actions Needed to Address Inadequate* (continued...)

Questions have been raised about DOD's ability to effectively manage contractors during contingency operations.[7] Some analysts assert that DOD has not adequately planned for the use of contractors, lacks contingency contracting experience, and does not sufficiently coordinate contracts across military services.[8] In January 2009, Secretary of Defense Roberts Gates acknowledged DOD's failure to adequately plan for the use of contractors, when he testified that use of contractors occurred

> without any supervision or without any coherent strategy on how we were going to do it and without conscious decisions about what we will allow contractors to do and what we won't allow contractors to do... We have not thought holistically or coherently about our use of contractors, particularly when it comes to combat environments or combat training.[9]

In 2007, a report by the Commission on Army Acquisition and Program Management in Expeditionary Operations (the Gansler Report) found that contracting officer representatives, who are responsible for managing contracts, usually have no prior experience with contractors and receive negligible training on how to manage contractors.[10] Some analysts and industry representatives argue that as a result, DOD is not getting the most out of the services provided by contractors in Afghanistan and Iraq.

Questions have also been raised about DOD spending on contractors. The Commission on Wartime Contracting highlighted over-spending on contracts as a key concern.[11] It reported that managerial shortages and limited oversight of contractors led to potentially unnecessary construction, such as a new $30 million dining facility to be completed a year before U.S. troops were required to leave Iraq, even though a then-recently upgraded dining facility was located nearby.[12]

Many analysts argue that only a culture shift in the military will improve contracting outcomes. The Gansler Report found that despite the importance of acquisitions to military performance,

> the Army apparently has not valued the skill and experience required to perform those processes ... without significant systemic change, the Army acquisition processes [contracting process] can be expected to inevitably return to below-mediocrity.[13]

(...continued)

Accountability over U.S. Efforts and Investments. GAO-08-568T. March 11, 2008. p. 4,6; See also Urgent Reform Required: Army Expeditionary Contracting, Op. Cit., p. 2.

[7] See U.S. Government Accountability Office, *High-Level DOD Action Needed to Address Long-standing Problems with Management and Oversight of Contractors Supporting Deployed Forces,* GAO-07-145, December 18, 2006.

[8] U.S. Government Accountability Office, *Contract Management: DOD Developed Draft Guidance for Operational Contract Support but Has Not Met All Legislative Requirements,* GAO-09-114R, November 20, 2008, p. 1.

[9] U.S. Congress, Senate Committee on Armed Services, *To Receive Testimony on the Challenges Facing the Department of Defense,* 110th Cong., 2nd sess., January 27, 2009.

[10] Commission on Army Acquisition and Program Management in Expeditionary Operations, *Urgent Reform Required: Army Expeditionary Contracting,* October 31, 2007, p. 43.

[11] Commission on Wartime Contracting: *Interim Findings and Path Forward,* 111th Cong., 1st sess., June 10, 2009; Commission on Wartime Contracting in Iraq and Afghanistan, *At What Cost? Contingency Contracting In Iraq and Afghanistan,* June 2009.

[12] Ibid, p. 52-54.

[13] Urgent Reform Required: Army Expeditionary Contracting, p. 9; see also New American Foundation, *Changing the Culture of Pentagon Contracting,* November 5, 2008.

Other analysts have argued that DOD's current approach to managing service contracts tends to be reactive and has not fully addressed key factors for success.[14] These analysts argue that to improve contracting outcomes, DOD must (1) understand how and why it uses contractors, including the number of contractors and types of services provided; (2) develop better management and contract oversight structures; and (3) establish and commit to a strategic approach that defines how contractors should be used to achieve operational success.

The use of contractors in Afghanistan and Iraq raises a number of issues for Congress, including (1) what role contractors should play in contingency operations, (2) whether DOD is gathering and analyzing the right data on the use of contractors, (3) what steps DOD is taking to improve contract management and oversight, and (4) the extent to which contractors are included in military doctrine and strategy. This report will discuss current contracting trends in Afghanistan and Iraq and steps DOD has taken to improve contractor oversight and management.

Contractors in the Central Command Region

Contractors supply a wide variety of services and products—including base support, construction, security, training local security forces, and transportation—to assist DOD operations in Afghanistan and Iraq.[15] While many of these contractors work in Afghanistan and Iraq, a number are also present in surrounding countries within the U.S. Central Command (CENTCOM) Area of Responsibility and in the United States.[16] For example, at Camp Arifjan, Kuwait, the Army relied on contractors to refurbish and repair vehicles used in Afghanistan and Iraq, such as the Bradley Fighting Vehicle and armored personnel carriers.[17]

DOD did not begin to gather and release data on contractors in CENTCOM until the second half of 2007. As a result, the following CRS analysis covers the period from September 2007 to December 2010. Contractor data in this report is based primarily on CENTCOM's quarterly manual census.

DOD is implementing the Synchronized Predeployment and Operational Tracker (SPOT), which is designed to track and monitor contractor personnel within a contingency operation. In January 2007, DOD chose SPOT as its primary system for collecting data on contractor personnel. In July 2008, DOD, the Department of State, and USAID signed a memorandum of understanding designating SPOT as the system to track contractor.[18] DOD originally planned to have SPOT replace the CENTCOM quarterly census as the tracking mechanism for contractor

---

[14] For example, see U.S. Government Accountability Office, *Defense Acquisitions: Tailored Approach Needed to Improve Service Acquisition Outcomes*, GAO-07-20, November 9, 2006, Highlights Page and p. 9.

[15] For a discussion on DOD's use of private security contractors in Iraq and Afghanistan, see CRS Report R40835, *The Department of Defense's Use of Private Security Contractors in Afghanistan and Iraq: Background, Analysis, and Options for Congress*, by Moshe Schwartz.

[16] USCENTCOM is responsible for operations in 20 countries in and around the Middle East including Afghanistan, Bahrain, Egypt, Iran, Iraq, Jordan, Kazakhstan, Kuwait, Kyrgyzstan, Lebanon, Oman, Pakistan, Qatar, Saudi Arabia, Syria, Tajikistan, Turkmenistan, U.A.E., Uzbekistan, and Yemen. The number of contractors based in the U.S. is small; these contractors are not included in this analysis.

[17] U.S. Government Accountability Office, *Defense Logistics: The Army Needs to Implement an Effective Management and Oversight Plan for the Equipment Maintenance Contract in Kuwait*, GAO-08-316R, January 22, 2008.

[18] DOD, Department of State, and USAID were required to sign a memorandum of understanding governing how to track contracts and contractor personnel in Iraq and Afghanistan. See P.L. 110-181, sec 861.

---

data by Q1 2010.[19] According to a recent GAO report, the transition to SPOT has been delayed and is expected to be completed no later than Q4 FY2011.[20]

A number of analysts have raised questions about the reliability of the data gathered by DOD. In October 2010, GAO reported that the quarterly contractor reports represent only a rough approximation of the number of contractors and therefore should not be relied upon for precise analysis.[21] GAO has also stated that because of data reliability issues, "caution should be used" when trying to use quarterly census data to identify trends or draw conclusions about the number of contractor personnel.[22] DOD officials have acknowledged data shortcomings and have stated that they are working to improve the reliability and the type of data gathered.[23] Reliable data on local nationals, particularly in Afghanistan, has been the most difficult to gather.[24] According to DOD

> The reported number of local national personnel in Afghanistan continues to fluctuate as we address reporting challenges. Specifically, there has been inconsistency in the reporting of day laborer personnel. SPOT [the Synchronized Predeployment and Operational Tracker system] does not require the registration of contractors working on a contract for less than 30 days. However, some contracting activities (in some quarters) include these contractors in their total manual census/SPOT Plus count. The inconsistency of who is counted is compounded by the frequent turnover of personnel responsible to provide input to the census and their individual understanding of reporting requirements. The issue was highlighted in the 4th quarter FY 2010 census. OSD has, in conjunction with USCENTCOM and the SPOT PM published guidance to clarify census reporting requirements.[25]

---

[19] August 23, 2009 version of CRS Report R40764, Department of Defense Contractors in Iraq and Afghanistan: Background and Analysis, by Moshe Schwartz, p. 4.

[20] According to GAO, as of October 2010, SPOT "still cannot reliably track information on contracts, assistance instruments, and associated personnel in Iraq or Afghanistan." See U.S. Government Accountability Office, *Contingency Contracting :Further Improvements in Agency Tracking of Contractor personnel and Contracts in Iraq and Afghanistan*, GAO-10-187, November 2, 2009; U.S. Government Accountability Office, *Contingency Contracting: DOD, State, and USAID Continue to Face Challenges in Tracking Contractor Personnel and Contracts in Iraq and Afghanistan* , GAO-10-1, October 1, 2009.

[21] U.S. Government Accountability Office, *Iraq and Afghanistan: DOD, State and USAID Face Continued Challenges in Tracking Contracts, Assistance Instruments, and Associated Personnel*, GAO-11-1, October 1, 2010, p. 18; See also, U.S. Government Accountability Office, *Contingency Contracting: DOD, State, and USAID Contracts and Contractor Personnel in Iraq and Afghanistan*, GAO-09-19, October 1, 2008, p. 6.

[22] U.S. Government Accountability Office, *Iraq and Afghanistan: DOD, State and USAID Face Continued Challenges in Tracking Contracts, Assistance Instruments, and Associated Personnel*, GAO-11-1, October 1, 2010, p. 4.

[23] Ibid. See also DOD US CENTCOM FY2009 2nd Quarter Contractor Census Report.

[24] Based on email correspondence with DOD official, received by CRS on January 18, 2011. Commenting on the unique difficulty in tracking Afghan local nationals, a DOD official wrote "many Afghan local nationals contracted by the U.S. government do not need to access U.S. controlled facilities or data systems and therefore, they do not require a base access card or a Letter of Authorization. Without these enforcement mechanisms, the ability to capture information about this population in the automated system is significantly challenged. Literacy challenges and the lack of identity documentation in Afghanistan further complicate the issue. Only now is the Afghan government starting to use biometrics."

[25] Based on email correspondence with DOD official, received by CRS on January 18, 2011.

Contractors in CENTCOM

Number of Contractors

According to DOD, as of March 31, 2011, there were approximately 174,000 DOD contractor personnel in the CENTCOM AOR compared to approximately 214,000 uniformed personnel in the region who are supporting operations in Afghanistan and Iraq.[26] Contractors made up 45% of DOD's combined contractor and uniformed personnel workforce in the CENTCOM AOR,[27] representing a .81:1 ratio between contractors and uniformed personnel (see **Table 1**).

Table 1. Comparison of Contractor Personnel to Troop Levels

(As of March 2011)

	Contractors	Troops	Ratio
Afghanistan Only	90,339	99,800	.91:1
Iraq Only	64,253	45,660	1.41:1
CENTCOM AOR	173,644	214,000	.81:1

Source: CENTCOM 2nd Quarter FY 2011 Contractor Census Report; Troop data from Joint Chiefs of Staff, "Boots on the Ground" January report to Congress.

Notes: CENTCOM AOR includes figures for Afghanistan and Iraq. CENTCOM troop level adjusted by CRS to exclude troops deployed to non-Central Command locations (e.g., Djibouti, Philippines, Egypt). Troop levels for non-CENTCOM locations are from DMDC, DRS 11280, "Location Report" for June 2010.

The number of contractor personnel in the CENTCOM AOR roughly tracks to the number of troops (see **Figure 2**).

---

[26] According to DOD, as of December 2010, there were 213,105 troops dedicated to supporting operations in Iraq and Afghanistan, of which approximately 3,700 were based outside of the CENTCOM region (Djibouti, Kenya, Ethiopia, and the Philippines). We subtracted the 3,700 personnel from the total number of troops to approximate the number of troops based in the CENTCOM region. This adjustment was made for all prior CENTCOM AOR troop levels. See Boots on Ground report to Congress. Data from Djibouti, Kenya, Ethiopia, and the Philippines is drawn from the "Average Number of Members deployed on any given day by Service Component and Month/Year" and the "Location Report", dated June 2010, which is the most recent data available to CRS.

[27] For purposes of this report, DOD's workforce is defined as uniformed personnel and the contractor workforce. DOD civilian personnel are excluded from this count. According to DOD's *Joint Personnel Status Report*, as of September 8, 2009, the DOD civilian workforce in Iraq was 2,033 (less than 1.0% of the total force) and the DOD civilian workforce in Afghanistan was 1,706 (less than 1.0% of the total force).

Figure 2. Number of Contractor Personnel in CENTCOM vs. Troop Levels

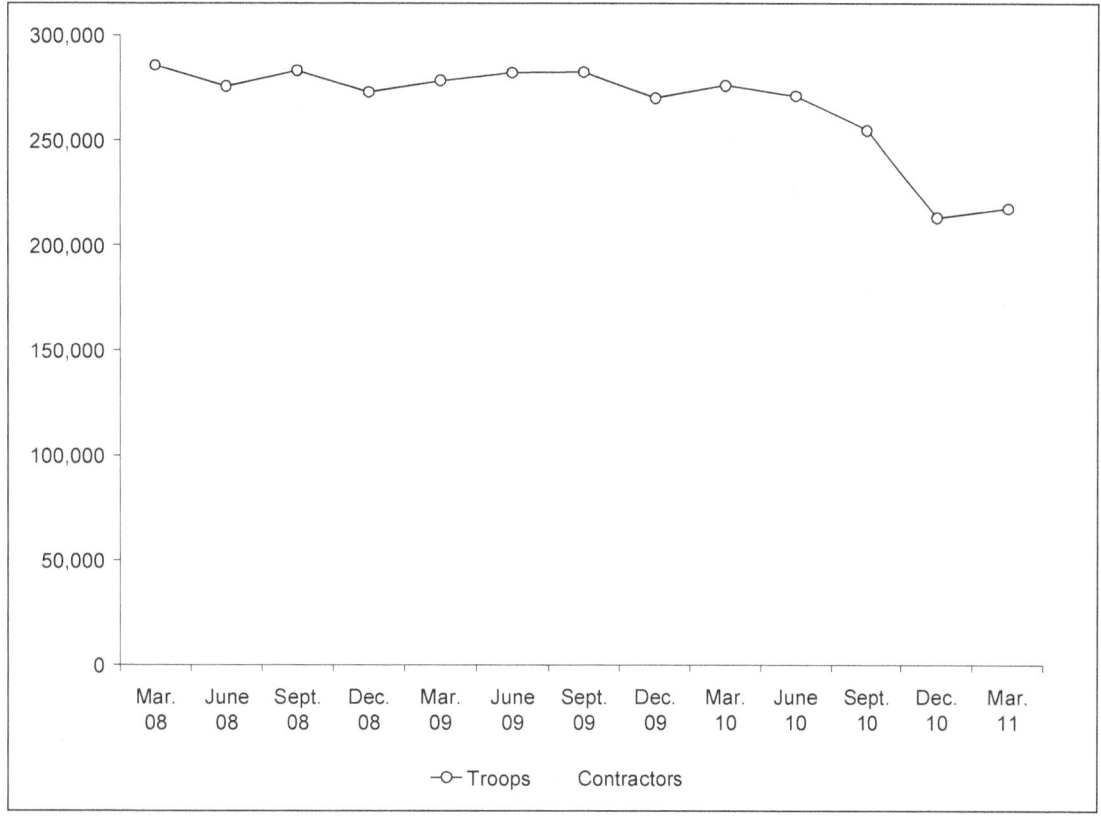

Source: CENTCOM Quarterly Contractor Census Reports. For troop levels, see Defense Manpower Data Center (DMDC), DRS 21198, "Average Number of Members deployed on any given day by Service Component and Month/Year," June 2010; DMDC, DRS 11280, "Location Report". Troop level data for December 2010 and March 2011 based on Boots on Ground Report to Congress because DMDC data was not available.

Notes: Historic troop level data based on data provided by DOD in June 2010. Troop levels for prior months are adjusted in successive reports and therefore may differ from earlier or subsequent DOD and CRS reports.

According to GAO, lessons learned and data analysis from past operations must be included in the development of a strategic plan to define contractor involvement in future operations.[28] Many analysts agree that understanding the role contractors play in various DOD operations—including the relationship between contractors and troop levels—could help to more effectively determine contractor support requirements in Afghanistan and Iraq, as well as future operations.

According to DOD, contracting with local nationals is an important element in counter-insurgency strategy.[29] Employing local nationals injects money into the local economy, provides job training, builds support among local nationals, and can give the U.S. a more sophisticated understanding of the local landscape, says DOD. In January 2009, General Raymond Odierno issued a memorandum to this effect, stating "employment of Iraqis not only saves money but it

---

[28] U.S. Government Accountability Office, Iraq and Afghanistan: Availability of Forces, Equipment, and Infrastructure Should Be Considered in Developing U.S. Strategy and Plans, GAO-09-380T, February 12, 2009.

[29] Based on discussions with DOD officials, July 23, 2009.

also strengthens the Iraqi economy and helps eliminate the root causes of the insurgency—poverty and lack of economic opportunity."[30] The memorandum set forth a goal of increasing the percentage of local national contractors. Despite this policy, DOD has trended away from using local nationals as contractor personnel in Afghanistan and Iraq. The percentage of contractors who were local nationals in both countries dropped from 49% in December 2009 to 36% in March 2011.

An analysis of contractor data also appears to indicate differences in how DOD used contractors in Afghanistan when compared to Iraq. For example, 51% of contractors in Afghanistan are local nationals compared to only 15% in Iraq (see **Figure 5** and **Figure 11**, respectively). Some analysts contend that understanding these differences—and why they occur—could help DOD to strategically plan for the management and use of contractors in future operations. For example, had DOD understood the extent to which it would rely on private security contractors in Afghanistan and Iraq, DOD might have put in place a more robust oversight and coordination mechanism earlier.[31]

DOD Contract Obligations

According to the Federal Procurement Data System – Next Generation (FPDS), DOD obligated approximately $27.2 billion on contracts in the Afghanistan and Iraq theaters of operations in FY2010, representing 17% of DOD's total war obligations in the Afghanistan and Iraq theaters of operations.[32] From FY2005 through FY2010, DOD obligated approximately $146 billion on contracts in the Iraq and Afghanistan theaters of operations (see **Figure 3**), representing 18% of total war spending for operations in Afghanistan and Iraq.[33]

---

[30] General Raymond T. Odierno, Memorandum, *Increased Employment of Iraq Citizens Through Command Contracts*, Multi-National Force-Iraq, January 31, 2009.

[31] In addition, a number of military bases in Iraq were not large enough to house contractors because DOD did not originally know how many contractors would be deployed with the military. As a result, DOD had to quickly find alternative housing for these contractors, which resulted in increased costs for DOD. Based on discussions with DOD officials, July 23, 2009.

[32] Based on total obligations of approximately $146 billion. Data includes total war-related obligations by year incurred (with classified request based on appropriations), based on data provided by the Defense Finance and Accounting Service. Classified appropriations allocated 60% to Iraq operations and 40% to Afghanistan operations. See CRS Report RL33110, *The Cost of Iraq, Afghanistan, and Other Global War on Terror Operations Since 9/11*, by Amy Belasco. When using this data, it is important to recognize the limitations of FPDS. GAO, CBO, and SIGIR have all raised concerns over the accuracy and reliability of the data contained in FPDS. Given these concerns, data from FPDS is used in this report only to identify broad trends and rough estimations.

[33] Based on total obligations of approximately $805 billion. Data for contract expenditures in both operations was retrieved from FPDS–NG. Data includes total war-related obligations by year incurred (with classified request based on appropriations), based on data provided by the Defense Finance and Accounting Service. Classified appropriations allocated 60% to Iraq operations and 40% to Afghanistan operations. The percentage of contract expenditures for operations in Afghanistan and Iraq from FY2005 through FY2010 were 22%, 22%, 15%, 17%, 18%, and 17%, respectively.

Figure 3. Contract Action Obligations for Iraq and Afghanistan Theaters

(In millions of dollars)

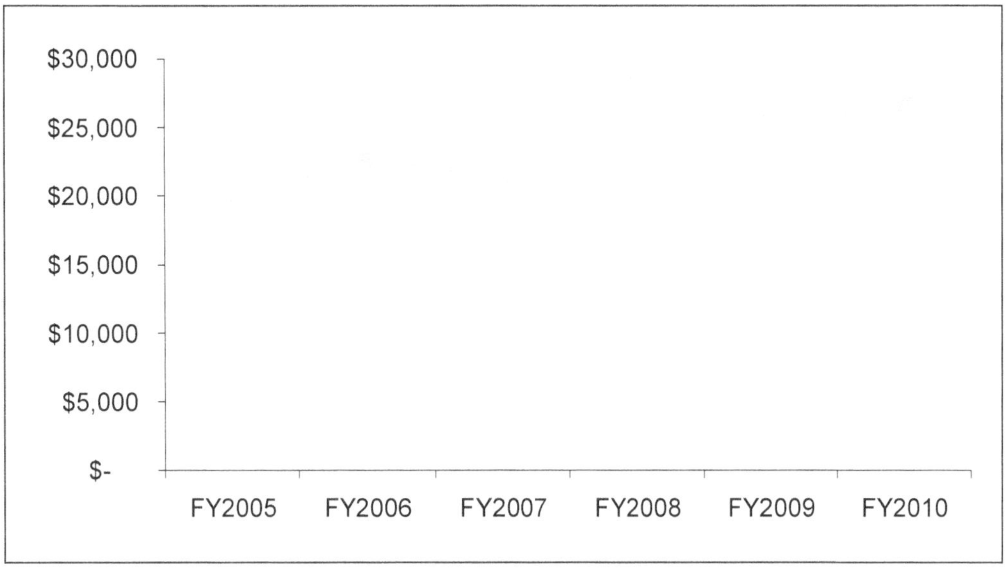

Source: FPDS-NG, January 26, 2011, for FY2005-FY2010.

Notes: Some of the contracts performed in countries categorized as being in the Iraqi theater support operations in both Iraq and Afghanistan.

Contractors in Afghanistan

Number of Contractors

As reflected in **Table 1**, according to DOD, as of March 2011, there were 90,339 DOD contractor personnel in Afghanistan, compared to approximately 99,800 uniformed personnel. Contractors made up 48% of DOD's workforce in Afghanistan (see **Figure 4**). This compares to December 2008, when contractors represented 69% of DOD's workforce in Afghanistan. [34]

---

[34] The number of contractors in Afghanistan in December 2008 represents the highest recorded percentage of contractors used by DOD in any conflict in the history of the United States. See CRS Report R40057, *Training the Military to Manage Contractors During Expeditionary Operations: Overview and Options for Congress*, by Moshe Schwartz.

Figure 4. Number of Contractor Personnel in Afghanistan vs. Troop Levels

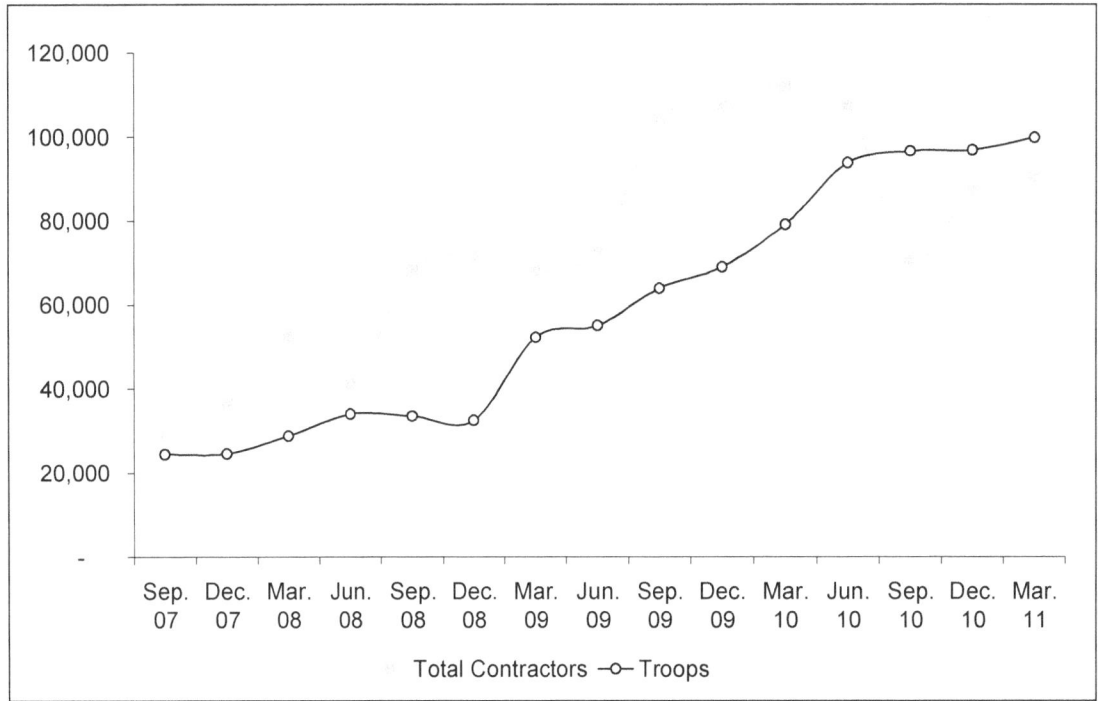

Source: CENTCOM Quarterly Census Reports; *Troop Levels in the Afghan and Iraq Wars, FY2001-FY2012: Cost and Other Potential Issues*, by Amy Belasco; Joint Staff, Joint Chiefs of Staff, "Boots on the Ground" monthly reports to Congress.

Type of Work Performed by Contractors

DOD does not report the breakdown of services that contractors provide in Afghanistan, with the exception of data on private security contractors. Nevertheless, the types of services provided by contractors in Afghanistan are similar to those conducted in Iraq, including logistics, construction, linguistic services, and transportation; the percentage of contractors providing each service is likely different.[35] DOD officials have stated in the past that they will start providing data on the breakdown of services in Afghanistan. However, to date, they have not done so.

Profile of Contractors

As of March 2011, of the approximately 90,000 contractors in Afghanistan, 20,000 were U.S. citizens, 24,000 were third-country nationals, and 46,000 were local nationals (see **Table 2**). Local nationals made up 51% of contractor personnel.

---

[35] The percentage of private security contractors operating in Iraq is different that of those operating in Afghanistan. See CRS Report R40835, *The Department of Defense's Use of Private Security Contractors in Afghanistan and Iraq: Background, Analysis, and Options for Congress*, by Moshe Schwartz.

Table 2. Contractor Personnel in Afghanistan

(As of March 2011)

	Total Contractors	U.S. Citizens	Third-Country Nationals	Local Nationals
Number	90,339	20,413	23,537	46,389
Percent of Total	100%	23%	26%	51%

Source: CENTCOM 2nd Quarter FY2011 Contractor Census Report.

As discussed above, the number of local nationals in recent census reports continues to fluctuate as DOD works to "address the challenges associated with the day to day employment of individual [local national] contractors."

In September 2010, General Petraeus, Commander of the International Security Assistance Force/United States Forces—Afghanistan, wrote that US and NATO forces must "[H]ire Afghans first, buy Afghan products, and build Afghan capacity"[36] Based on the available data, DOD uses more local nationals in Afghanistan than U.S. citizens and third-country nationals combined. However, the percentage of contractor personnel who are local nationals has steadily declined from a high of 86% in September 2008 to a low of 51% in March 2011 (see **Figure 5**), despite DOD's policy of trying to hire local nationals.

---

[36] General David H. Petraeus, *COMISAF's Counterinsurgency (COIN) Contracting Guidance*, International Security Assistance Force/United States Forces - Afghanistan, September 8, 2010, p. 1.

Figure 5. Contractor Personnel Trends in Afghanistan by Nationality

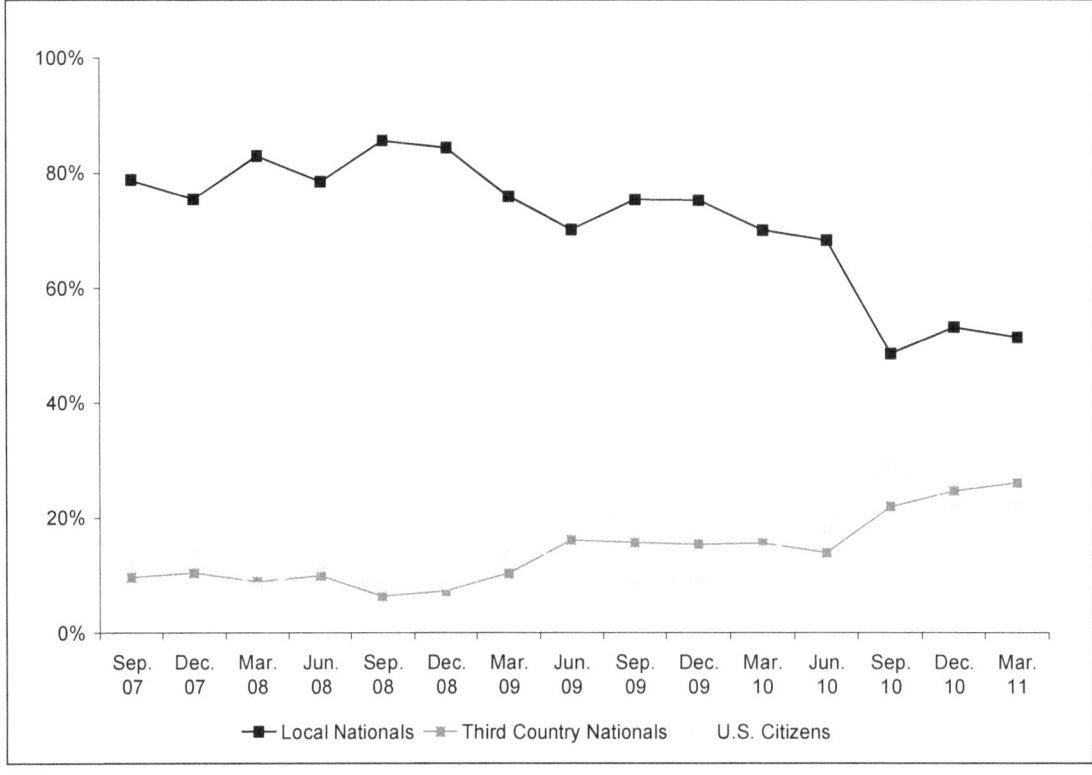

Source: CENTCOM Quarterly Contractor Census Reports.

Pursuing an Afghan First policy raises a number of issues. For example, focusing on the nationality of contractor personnel, and not where in Afghanistan workers are from, can undermine some of the goals of the Afghan first policy. When contractors are working in a given region, the local population often wants local residents to be hired to perform the work. In such situations, bringing in Afghan contractors who are not from the local community could undermine efforts to build relationships with the local populace. Another issue to consider is whether in certain circumstances awarding contracts to local nationals could empower bad actors, criminal gangs, or corrupt individuals. In those instances, it may be preferable to award a contract to foreign companies.

The International Security Assistance Force (ISAF) has generally had little visibility into who the local national contractors and subcontractors are who work for DOD, including not knowing the extent to which money from government contracts is empowering bad actors or groups whose interests run counter to the mission of coalition partners.[37]

One of NATO-ISAF's objectives is to reduce corruption and neutralize "criminal patronage networks."[38] In an effort to address corruption, ISAF established the Combined Joint Interagency Task Force (CJIATF) Shafafiyat (which means 'transparency' in Dari and Pashto) in August 2010

---

[37] CDR Mark Runstrom, SC, USN, Joint Staff J-4, Chief, Operational Contract Support, *Joint Staff OCS Update*, Joint Staff, PowerPoint Presentation, July 2010.

[38] NATO ISAF, *Shafafiyat – Transparency 101*, PowerPoint Presentation, April 2011.

under the leadership of Brigadier General H.R. McMaster to address the issue of corruption.[39] Under CJIATF Shafafiyat are three specialized units: Task Force Spotlight (focused on private security companies), Task Force 2010 (focused on the risk of contracting funds going to hostile groups), and CJIATF Nexus (focused on the link between drug traffickers, insurgents, and corrupt powerbrokers). CJIATF Nexus operates in the south and southwest of Afghanistan.[40]

DOD Contract Obligations

According to FPDS, DOD obligated approximately $11.8 billion on contracts in the Afghanistan theater of operations in FY2010, representing 15% of total obligations in the Afghanistan in the area.[41] From FY2005-FY2010, DOD obligated approximately $33.9 billion on contracts primarily in the Afghanistan theater, representing 16% of total DOD obligations for operations in that area (see **Figure 6**. For a breakout of contract obligations see **Table C-1**).[42]

---

[39] Department of Defense, *Report to Congress on Progress Toward Security and Stability in Afghanistan*, November 2010.

[40] CJIATF Shafafiyat also maintains a coordinating relationship with the Afghan Threat Finance Cell (which investigates illicit financing) and the Interagency Operations Coordination Center (which investigates links to drug trafficking).

[41] Based on total obligations of $79.4 billion. Data includes total war-related obligations by year incurred (with classified request based on appropriations), based on data provided by the Defense Finance and Accounting Service. Classified appropriations allocated 60% to Iraq operations and 40% to Afghanistan operations. See CRS Report RL33110, *The Cost of Iraq, Afghanistan, and Other Global War on Terror Operations Since 9/11*, by Amy Belasco.

[42] Based on total obligations of $216.4 billion. Data includes total war-related obligations by year incurred (with classified request based on appropriations), based on data provided by the Defense Finance and Accounting Service. Classified appropriations allocated 60% to Iraq operations and 40% to Afghanistan operations. See CRS Report RL33110, *The Cost of Iraq, Afghanistan, and Other Global War on Terror Operations Since 9/11*, by Amy Belasco. The percentage of contract expenditures for operations in Afghanistan from FY2005 through FY2010 were 12%, 16%, 16%, 19%, 16%, and 15% respectively.

Figure 6. Contract Action Obligations for Afghanistan Theater

(In millions of dollars)

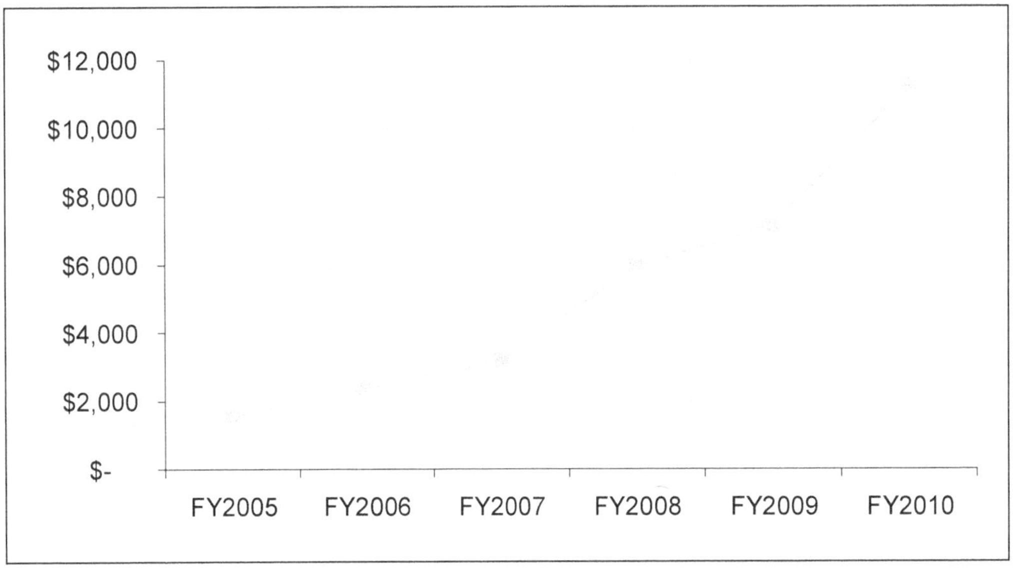

Source: FPDS-NG, January 26, 2011, for FY2005-FY2010.

Notes: For purposes of this analysis, the Afghan theater includes: Afghanistan, Kazakhstan, Kyrgyzstan, Pakistan, Tajikistan, Turkmenistan, and Uzbekistan. Some contracts performed in countries in the Afghan theater also support operations in Iraq. Conversely, some contracts performed in countries in the Iraqi theater support operations in Afghanistan. Due to data limitations, obligations for contracts performed in a given country can not be accurately allocated between operations in Iraq and Afghanistan.

Contractors in Iraq

Number of Contractors

As reflected in **Table 1** (above), according to DOD, as of March 2011, there were approximately 64,000 DOD contractor personnel in Iraq compared to 46,000 uniformed personnel in-country. Contractors made up approximately 58% of DOD's workforce in Iraq. Both contractor and troop levels have decreased every quarter for more than two years (see **Figure 7**).

Figure 7. Number of Contractor Personnel in Iraq vs. Troop Levels

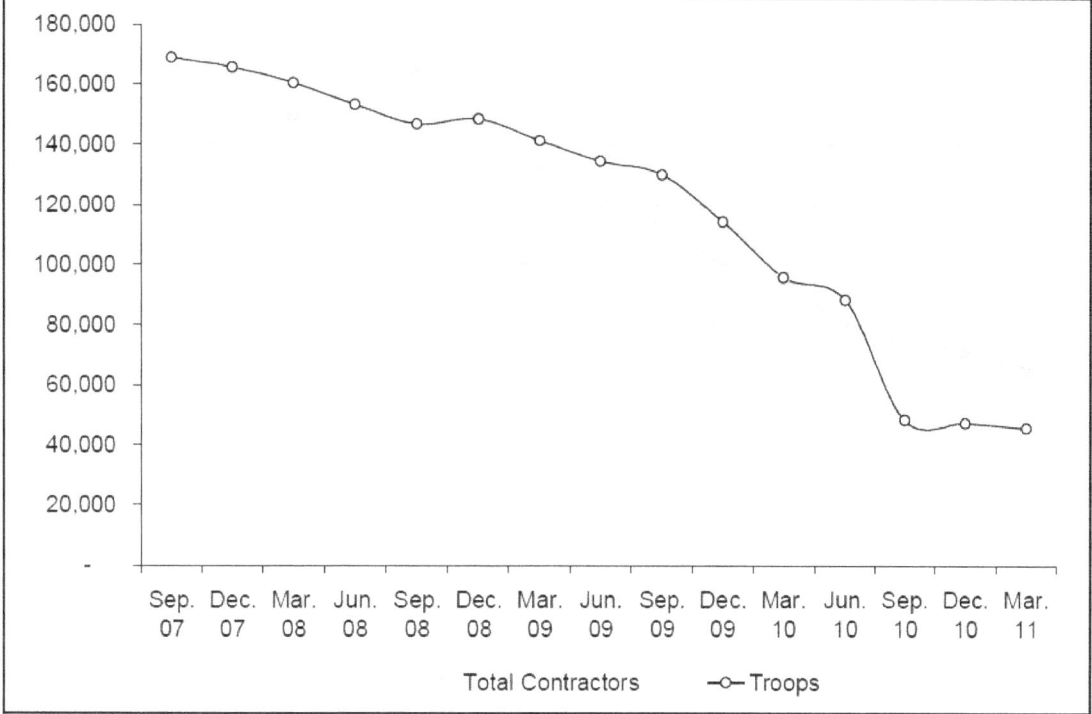

Source: CENTCOM Quarterly Census Reports; Joint Staff, Joint Chiefs of Staff, "Boots on the Ground" monthly reports to Congress.

Notes: The y-intercept for the level of troops and contractor personnel is similar. The R^2 value for the linear trend line for contractor personnel is 0.93 and for uniformed personnel is .91. R^2 is a statistical term used to describe the goodness of the fit between the trend line and the data points. R^2 is a descriptive measure between 0 and 1. The closer the R^2 value is to one, the better the fit of the trend line to the data.

Type of Work Performed by Contractors

Contractors perform a wide range of services in Iraq. As of March 2011, approximately 39,000 personnel (61% of contractors) performed base support functions such as maintaining the grounds, running dining facilities, and performing laundry services (see **Figure 8**). Security was the second most common service provided, with approximately 10,500 personnel (16% of contractors). Combined, these two categories accounted for almost 80% of DOD contractors in Iraq.

Figure 8. Contractor Personnel in Iraq by Type of Service Provided

(As of March 2011)

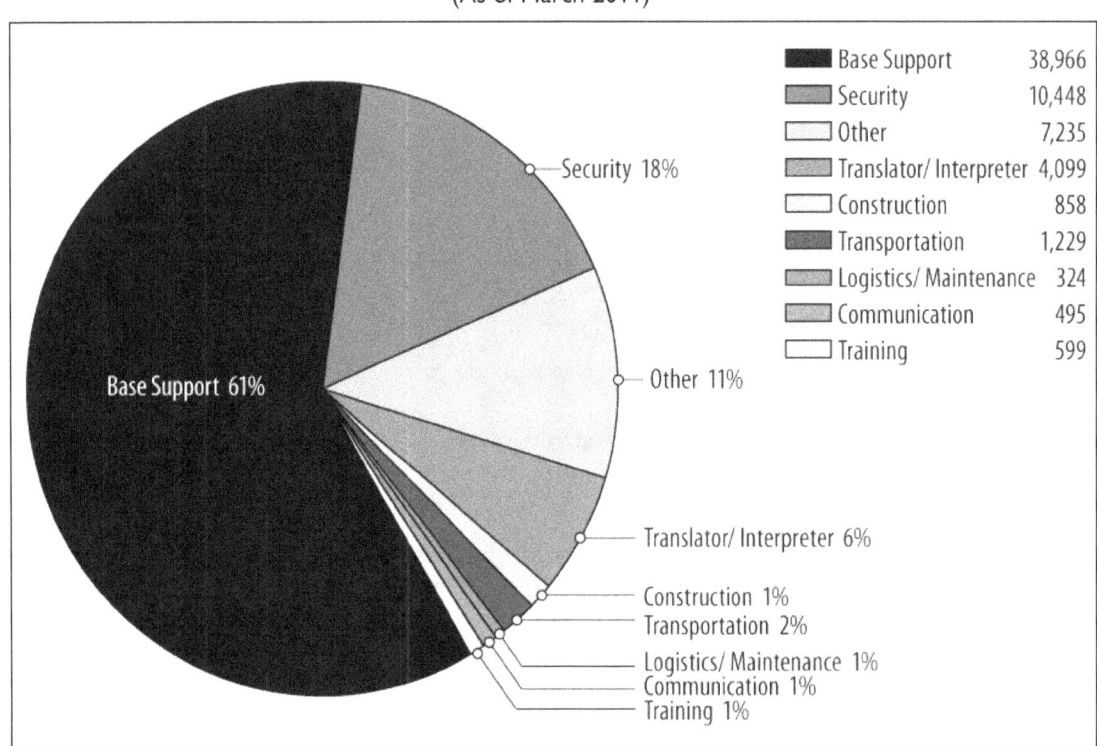

■ Base Support		38,966
▨ Security		10,448
▢ Other		7,235
▨ Translator/ Interpreter		4,099
▢ Construction		858
▨ Transportation		1,229
▨ Logistics/ Maintenance		324
▨ Communication		495
▢ Training		599

Security 18%

Base Support 61%

Other 11%

Translator/ Interpreter 6%

Construction 1%
Transportation 2%
Logistics/ Maintenance 1%
Communication 1%
Training 1%

Source: DOD US CENTCOM 2nd Quarter FY2011 Contractor Census Report.

Notes: Numbers may vary slightly from data in other sections of the report due to differences in the points in time when data was gathered. The Department of Defense did not separately track Logistics/Maintenance or Training until the first quarter of 2010.

As the overall number of troops in Iraq has decreased, so too has the overall number of contractors. For example, since June 2008, as troop levels dropped by approximately 108,000 (70%), total contractors fell by approximately 95,000 (60%). However, as reflected in **Appendix A**, the number of contractors did not decrease uniformly across the contractor workforce. For example, during the same period, contractors providing base support and construction declined by 57% (51,000 personnel) and 98% (35,000 personnel) respectively, whereas the number of contractors providing security actually increased by 14% (1,000 personnel).

This data indicates that as the services required by DOD change during the course of operations, the percentages and numbers of contractors providing different types of services also change. The drop in the number of contractor personnel performing base support and construction is a reflection of DOD's shrinking footprint and winding down of reconstruction activities. As reflected in **Figure 9**, the percentage of contractors performing base support has remained relatively constant, the percentage working in construction has decreased, and the percentage performing security has increased.

Figure 9. Percent of Contractor Personnel Performing Types of Service in Iraq

(As of March 2011)

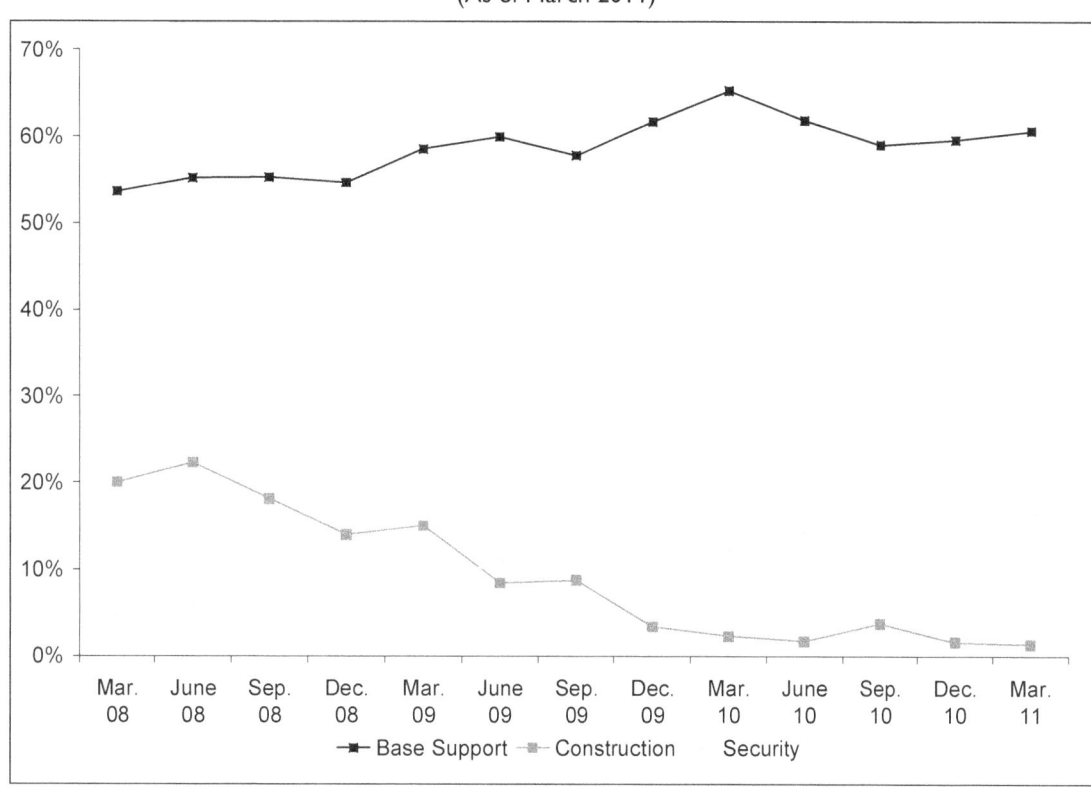

Source: CENTCOM Quarterly Census Reports.

Profile of Contractors

Of the approximately 64,000 contractors in Iraq as of March 2011, some 18,000 were U.S. citizens, 9,000 were local nationals, and 37,000 were third-country nationals (see **Table 3**). Third-country nationals made up more than half of all contractor personnel.

Table 3. Contractor Personnel in Iraq

(As of March 2011)

	Total Contractors	U.S. Citizens	Third-Country Nationals	Local Nationals
Number	64,258	18,393	36,523	9,337
Percent of Total	100%	29%	57%	15%

Source: CENTCOM 2nd Quarter FY2011 Contractor Census Report. Percentages do not equal 100% due to rounding.

From June 2008 to March 2011, the number of Iraqi contractor personnel dropped by almost 61,000 (87%), while the number of U.S. personnel decreased by 8,000 (31%) (see **Figure 10**).

This can be only partially explained by the drop in the number of contractor personnel performing construction; local nationals generally represent more than 80% of these workers.

Figure 10. Number of Contractor Personnel in Iraq by Nationality

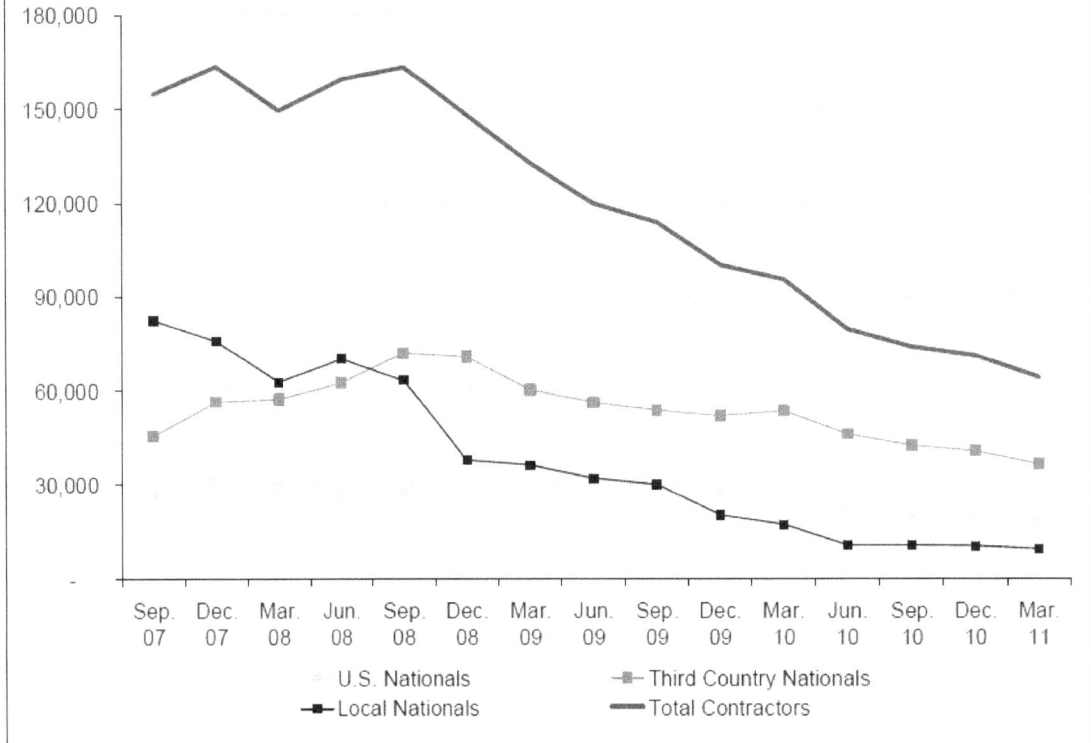

Source: CENTCOM Quarterly Contractor Census Reports.

The percentage of contractors who are local nationals has steadily dropped from a high of 53% in September 2007 (see **Figure 11**). This drop has occurred despite a DOD policy to increase the percentage of local national contractors.[43]

---

[43] General Raymond T. Odierno, Memorandum, Increased Employment of Iraq Citizens Through Command Contracts, Multi-National Force-Iraq, January 31, 2009.

Figure 11. Contractor Personnel Trends in Iraq by Nationality

(As percentage of total contractor workforce)

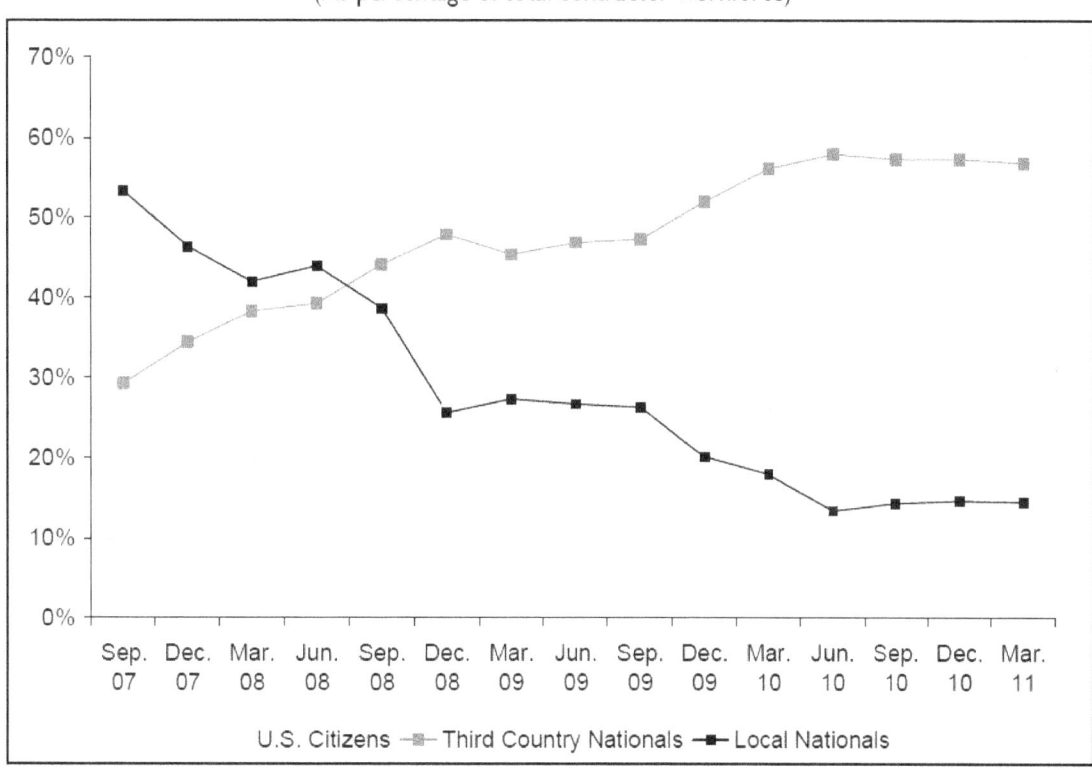

Source: CRS analysis of DOD data as contained in CENTCOM Quarterly Censuses.

DOD Contract Obligations

DOD obligated approximately $15.4 billion on contracts in the Iraq theater of operations in FY2010, representing 20% of total spending in those regions. [44] From FY2005 to FY2010, DOD obligated approximately $112.8 billion on contracts primarily in the Iraq theater of operations, representing 19% of total obligations for operations in Iraq. [45]

---

[44] Based on total obligations of $76.6 billion. Data includes total war-related obligations by year incurred (with classified request based on appropriations), based on data provided by the Defense Finance and Accounting Service. Classified appropriations allocated 60% to Iraq operations and 40% to Afghanistan operations. See CRS Report RL33110, *The Cost of Iraq, Afghanistan, and Other Global War on Terror Operations Since 9/11*, by Amy Belasco.

[45] Based on total obligations of $588.6 billion. Data includes total war-related obligations by year incurred (with classified request based on appropriations), based on data provided by the Defense Finance and Accounting Service. Classified appropriations allocated 60% to Iraq operations and 40% to Afghanistan operations. See CRS Report RL33110, *The Cost of Iraq, Afghanistan, and Other Global War on Terror Operations Since 9/11*, by Amy Belasco. The percentage of contract expenditures for operations in Iraq from FY2005 through FY2009 were 24%, 23%, 15%, 17%, 20%, and 20%, respectively.

Figure 12. Contract Action Obligations for Iraq Area of Operations

(In millions of dollars)

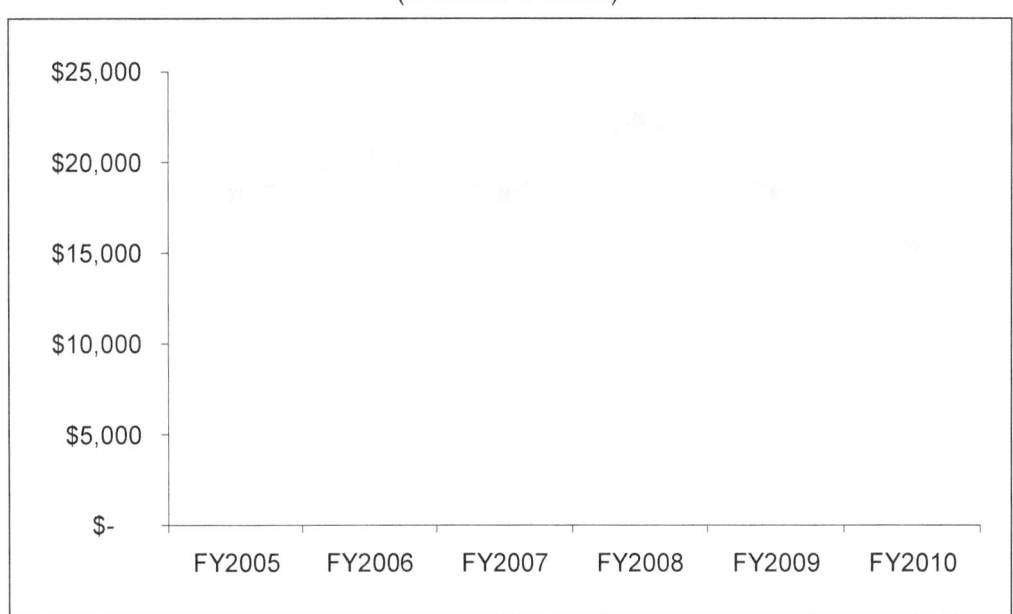

Source: FPDS-NG, January 26, 2011, for FY2005-FY2010.

Notes: Based on Congressional Budget Office methodology, the Iraqi theater includes: Iraq, Bahrain, Jordan, Kuwait, Oman, Qatar, Saudi Arabia, Turkey, and the United Arab Emirates. See Congressional Budget Office, *Contractors' Support of U.S. Operations in Iraq,* August 2008, p. 3.

Some contracts performed in countries in the Afghan theater also support operations in Iraq. Conversely, some contracts performed in countries in the Iraqi theater support operations in Afghanistan. Due to data limitations, obligations for contracts performed in a given country can not be accurately allocate between operations in Iraq and Afghanistan.

Data listed above differs from data reported by CBO and GAO due primarily to differences in methodology. For a detailed discussion of differences in CRS, CBO, and GAO data and methodology, see **Appendix C**.

Efforts to Improve Contractor Management and Oversight

In January 2009, Secretary Defense Robert Gates testified that contractors were used in Iraq "without any supervision or without any coherent strategy on how we were going to do it and without conscious decisions about what we will allow contractors to do and what we won't allow contractors to do …and those are the areas that I think especially we need to focus on first."[46]

In light of DOD's experiences in Afghanistan and Iraq, and in response to legislation and the findings of numerous studies (including the Gansler Report, GAO reports, and Special Inspector General for Iraq Reconstruction reports), DOD has taken a number of steps to try to improve how

---

[46] U.S. Congress, Senate Committee on Armed Services, *Challenges Facing the Department of Defense*, 111th Cong., 1st sess., January 27, 2009.

it manages contractors in Afghanistan and Iraq. These efforts have included organizational changes such as setting up the Joint Contracting Command to provide a more centralized contracting support and management system;[47] implementing regulatory and policy changes aimed at improving management;[48] improving training for uniformed personnel on how to manage contractors;[49] and increasing the size of the acquisition workforce in theater.[50]

DOD senior officials are also making a concerted effort to elevate the importance of contracting and think about the role of contractors during contingency operations. In a September 2010 memorandum to commanders, contracting personnel, uniformed personnel, and civilians in Afghanistan, General Petraeus, Commander of the International Security Assistance Force/United States Forces—Afghanistan, stated that "contracting has to be a 'commander's business.'"[51] This statement is consistent with the efforts of other senior leaders, including the Chairman of the Joint Chiefs of Staff's establishment of a task force on contractor reliance in contingency operations and Secretary Gates' testimony.

A number of these initiatives have been reflected in or were the result of legislation. For example, the Joint Contingency Acquisition Support Office was established as a result of section 854 of the FY2007 John Warner National Defense Authorization Act (NDAA) requiring DOD to create a team of contingency contracting experts that can be deployed to support military operations.[52] In the FY2008 NDAA, Congress mandated contingency contracting training for non-acquisition military personnel who will have relevant contracting responsibilities.[53]

A number of analysts and government officials believe that some of these efforts have improved DOD's ability to manage and oversee contractors in Afghanistan and Iraq. For example, in Iraq, DOD established Contractor Operations Cells to coordinate the movement of PSCs and the Armed Contractor Oversight Directorate to manage PSCs.[54] The improvements in how DOD

---

[47] USCENTCOM, 2nd Quarterly Contractor Census Report, p. 4, May, 2009.

[48] These changes include establishing DOD Directive 3020.40 - *Orchestrating, Synchronizing, and Integrating Program Management of Contingency Acquisition Planning and its Operational Execution* on March 24, 2009 (assigns program management responsibilities for acquisitions in contingency operations) and creating the Operational Contract Support Concept of Operations signed on March 31, 2010.

[49] DOD is developing an on-line course that offers pre-deployment training to personnel about planning for and working with contractors during military operations. Additionally, the Army continues to develop informational handbooks to help guide military personnel who work with contractors regarding the contracting process and their specific roles and responsibilities when coordinating with contractors.

[50] USCENTCOM, 2nd Quarterly Contractor Census Report, p. 15, May, 2009.

[51] General David H. Petraeus, *COMISAF's Counterinsurgency (COIN) Contracting Guidance*, International Security Assistance Force/United States Forces - Afghanistan, September 8, 2010, p. 1.

[52] P.L. 109-364, Sec. 854.

[53] P.L. 110-181 Sec. 849.

[54] The Armed Contractor Oversight Division in Iraq was renamed the Armed Contractor Oversight Bureau. For a detailed discussion on DOD efforts to improve the coordination of PSC movements throughout Iraq, see Government Accountability Office, *REBUILDING IRAQ: DOD and State Department Have Improved Oversight and Coordination of Private Security Contractors in Iraq, but Further Actions Are Needed to Sustain Improvements*, GAO-08-966, July 31, 2008; Special Inspector General for Iraq Reconstruction, *Field Commanders See Improvements in Controlling and Coordinating Private Security Contractor Missions in Iraq*, SIGIR 09-022, July 28, 2009. Commission on Wartime Contracting in Iraq and Afghanistan, *At What Cost? Contingency Contracting in Iraq and Afghanistan*, Interim Report, June 2009, p. 73.

---

manages PSCs in Iraq have been noted by the Special Inspector General for Iraq Reconstruction, the Commission on Wartime Contracting, and the GAO.[55]

Despite these efforts, DOD still faces challenges in managing contractors. As an April 2010 Joint Staff report stated, "[A]lthough progress has been made in the past 4 years to improve operational contract support (OCS) policy and doctrine, significant challenges remain."[56] For example, DOD was recently criticized for not knowing who is receiving money from U.S.-funded contracts in Afghanistan. There have been allegations that money from U.S.-funded contracts has gone to local warlords and the Taliban.[57] Recent criticism also includes DOD's continued inability to accurately track contracts and contractor personnel in Afghanistan and Iraq.[58]

Selected Congressional Hearings and Legislation

Congress has held a number of hearings and passed legislation relating to DOD contracting efforts in Afghanistan and Iraq. Hearings have taken place in a number of different committees and have covered a wide array of related issues, including private security contractors, interrogators, logistic support, contract management and oversight, and training requirements. Congress has also passed legislation annually in a number of these areas. Such legislation generally occurs in the National Defense Authorization Act (NDAA). The following section provides a highlight of key congressional activity related to contingency contracting.

Private Security Contractors

Congress has focused more on private security contractors than other contracting issues, even though such contractors have generally comprised roughly 10-20% of DOD contractors in Afghanistan and Iraq. Hearings have been held in the Senate Committee on Armed Services,[59] the Senate Committee on Homeland Security and Governmental Affairs,[60] the House Committee on

---

[55] U.S. Special Inspector General for Iraq Reconstruction, *Field Commanders See Improvements in Controlling and Coordinating Private Security Contractor Missions in Iraq*, SIGIR 09-022, July 28, 2009; U.S. Congress, House Committee on Oversight and Government Reform, Subcommittee on National Security and Foreign Affairs, *Commission on Wartime Contracting: Interim Findings and Path Forward*, 111th Cong., 1st sess., June 10, 2009; U.S. Government Accountability Office, *REBUILDING IRAQ: DOD and State Department Have Improved Oversight and Coordination of Private Security Contractors in Iraq, but Further Actions Are Needed to Sustain Improvements*, GAO-08-966, July 31, 2008.

[56] Captain Peter G. Stamatopoulus, *Chairman of the Joint Chiefs of Staff Dependence on Contractor Support in Contingency Operations Task Force*, Department of Defense, Phase II: An Evaluation of the Range and Depth of Service Contract Capabilities in Iraq, April 30, 2010, p. 1.

[57] U.S. Congress, House Committee on Oversight and Government Reform, Subcommittee on National Security and Foreign Affairs, *Investigation of Protection Payments for Safe Passage along the Afghan Supply Chain*, 111th Cong., 2nd sess., June 22, 2010. See also Senate Armed Services Committee, "Inquiry into the Role and Oversight of Private Security Contractors in Afghanistan," October 7, 2010.

[58] U.S. Government Accountability Office, *Iraq and Afghanistan: DOD, State, and USAID Face Continued Challenges in Tracking Contracts, Assistance Instruments, and Associated Personnel*, 11-1, October 2010.

[59] U.S. Congress, Senate Committee on Armed Services, Inquiry into the Treatment of Detainees in U.S. Custody, 110th Cong., 1st sess., August 3, 2007.

[60] U.S. Congress, Senate Committee on Homeland Security and Governmental Affairs, *An Uneasy Relationship: U.S. Reliance on Private Security Firms in Overseas Operations*, 110th Cong., 2nd sess., February 27, 2008.

Oversight and Government Reform,[61] and the House Committee on Armed Services.[62] This issue was also raised in other hearings, such as the House Committee on Oversight and Government Reform's hearing on the *Commission on Wartime Contracting: Interim Findings and Path Forward*[63] and the House Committee on the Judiciary' hearing on *Enforcement of Federal Criminal Law to Protect Americans Working for U.S. Contractors in Iraq.*[64] The National Security and Foreign Affairs Subcommittee of the House Committee on Oversight and Government Reform conducted a hearing *Investigation of Protection Payments for Safe Passage along the Afghan Supply Chain,* which focused on armed private security contractors providing convoy security along the Afghan supply chain.[65] More recently, the Senate Armed Services Committee issued a report that found evidence of U.S.-funded prime contractors supporting the Taliban and subcontracting to warlords.[66]

In the FY2008 NDAA, Congress required the Secretary of Defense, in coordination with the Secretary of State, to prescribe regulations and guidance relating to screening, equipping, and managing private security personnel in areas of combat operations. These regulations were to include tracking private security personnel (PSC), authorizing and accounting for weapons used by PSCs, and reporting requirements whenever a security contractor discharges a weapon, kills or injures another person, or is killed or injured.[67] Included in the FY2009 NDAA is a "Sense of Congress" that private security contractors should not perform inherently governmental functions, such as security protection of resources, in high-threat operational environments.[68] In the same legislation, Congress mandated that interrogation is an inherently governmental function that DOD may not outsource to contractors.[69]

Contractors Training Local Security Forces

Congress has turned its attention to contractors training local security forces in Afghanistan and Iraq. Such hearings have raised a number of issues, including the behavior of such contactors, whether there is sufficient contract oversight, and the cost of such contracts. The Senate Committee on Armed Services held a hearing on *Contracting in a Counterinsurgency: An Examination of the Blackwater-Paravant Contract and the Need for Oversight,* which focused on

---

[61] U.S. Congress, House Committee on Oversight and Government Reform, *Private Security Contracting in Iraq and Afghanistan,* 110th Cong., 1st sess., October 2, 2007.

[62] U.S. Congress, House Committee on Armed Services, *Contingency Contracting: Implementing a Call for Urgent Reform,* 110th Cong., 2nd sess., April 9, 2008.

[63] U.S. Congress, House Committee on Oversight and Government Reform, Subcommittee on National Security and Foreign Affairs, *Commission on Wartime Contracting: Interim Findings and Path Forward,* 111th Cong., 1st sess., June 9, 2009.

[64] U.S. Congress, House Committee on the Judiciary, Subcommittee on Crime, Terrorism, and Homeland Security, *Enforcement of Federal Criminal Law to Protect Americans Working for U.S. Contractors in Iraq,* 110th Cong., 1st sess., December 19, 2007.

[65] U.S. Congress, House Committee on Oversight and Government Reform, Subcommittee on National Security and Foreign Affairs, *Investigation of Protection Payments for Safe Passage along the Afghan Supply Chain,* 111th Cong., 2nd sess., June 22, 2010.

[66] Senate Armed Services Committee, "Inquiry into the Role and Oversight of Private Security Contractors in Afghanistan," October 7, 2010.

[67] P.L. 110-181, sec 862.

[68] P.L. 110-417, sec 832.

[69] P.L. 110-417, sec 1057.

the shooting of Afghan civilians by two Paravant employees.[70] The Ad Hoc Subcommittee on Contracting Oversight of the Senate, Committee on Homeland Security and Governmental Affairs held a hearing *Afghan Police Force Training*, which raised the issue of waste and a lack of oversight on $6 billion spent on contracts to train the Afghan national police force.[71]

Contract Management, Oversight, and Coordination

Management and oversight of contracting personnel in contingency operations has been of significant interest to Congress. Hearings on these issues have been held in the Senate Committee on Armed Services[72] and the Senate Committee on Homeland Security and Governmental Affairs.[73] This issue was also raised by the House Committee on Armed Services' hearing on *Coordinating Contract Support on the Battlefield: Defense, State, and U.S. AID*[74] and the House Committee on Oversight and Government Reform's hearing on *Commission on Wartime Contracting: Interim Findings and Path Forward.*[75]

In the FY2008 NDAA, Congress mandated the creation of a memorandum of understanding between the Secretary of Defense, Secretary of State, and Administrator of the United States Agency for International Development to promote coordinated contingency contracting practices.[76] Congress also established the Commission on Wartime Contracting to study wartime contracting in Afghanistan and Iraq, determine the extent to which the federal government relies on contractors, and examine how U.S. objectives are achieved by this reliance on contractors.[77] In the FY2009 NDAA, Congress added additional requirements and reporting mechanisms for alleged crimes committed by or against contractor personnel in Iraq or Afghanistan.[78]

Training Contractors and the Military in Contingency Contracting

Some testimony at various hearings emphasized that increased training is necessary for non-acquisition personnel throughout the military.[79] Concerned that DOD contractors and personnel

---

[70] U.S. Congress, Senate Committee on Armed Services, *Contracting in a Counterinsurgency: An Examination of the Blackwater-Paravant Contract and the Need for Oversight*, 111th Cong., 2nd sess., February 24, 2010.

[71] U.S. Congress, Senate Committee on Homeland Security and Governmental Affairs, Ad Hoc Subcommittee on Contracting Oversight, *Contracts for Afghan National Police Training*, 111th Cong., 2nd sess., April 15, 2010.

[72] U.S. Congress, Senate Committee on Armed Services, Subcommittee on Readiness and Management Support, *To Receive Testimony on Department of Defense Contracting in Iraq and Afghanistan*, 110th Cong., 2nd sess., April 2, 2008.

[73] U.S. Congress, Senate Committee on Homeland Security and Governmental Affairs, Subcommittee on Federal Financial Management, Government Information, Federal Services, and International Security, *Management and Oversight of Contingency Contracting in Hostile Zones*, 110th Cong., 2nd sess., January 24, 2008.

[74] U.S. Congress, House Committee on Armed Services, Subcommittee on Oversight and Investigations, *Coordinating Contract Support on the Battlefield: Defense, State, and U.S. AID*, 111th Cong., 1st sess., April 1, 2009.

[75] U.S. Congress, House Committee on Oversight and Government Reform, Subcommittee on National Security and Foreign Affairs, *Commission on Wartime Contracting: Interim Findings and Path Forward*, 111th Cong., 1st sess., June 9, 2009.

[76] P.L. 110-181, sec 861.

[77] P.L. 110-181, sec 841.

[78] P.L. 110-417, sec 854.

[79] See U.S. Congress, House Committee on Armed Services, *Contingency Contracting: Implementing a Call for Urgent* (continued...)

are not sufficiently trained to execute contingency contracting, Congress passed legislation requiring DOD to implement training requirements for contingency contracting personnel (in coordination with the Secretary of Defense, the Chairman of the Joint Chiefs of Staff, and the Defense Acquisition University), and to provide specific training to contract management personnel.[80] In the FY2008 NDAA, Congress called for contract management training for personnel outside the acquisition workforce who are responsible for contractor oversight. The FY2008 NDAA also mandated the incorporation of contractors in mission-readiness exercises with uniformed personnel.[81] In addition, Congress passed legislation establishing of a government-wide Contingency Contracting Corps that will be available for deployment in responding to an emergency or major disasters, or a contingency operation.[82] Congress authorized this corps to receive specific training in contingency contracting.

(...continued)

Reform, 110th Cong., 2nd sess., April 10, 2008; U.S. Congress, House Committee on Oversight and Government Reform, Subcommittee on National Security and Foreign Affairs, *Commission on Wartime Contracting: Interim Findings and Path Forward*, 111th Cong., 1st sess., June 9, 2009; and U.S. Congress, House Committee on Armed Services, *Contingency Contracting: Has the Call for Urgent Reform been Answered?*, 111th Cong., 1st sess., March 25, 2009..

[80] P.L. 109-163, sec 817 and P.L. 109-364, sec 854.

[81] P.L. 110-181, sec 849

[82] P.L. 110-417, sec. 870

Appendix A. Contractor Personnel in Iraq by Type of Service Provided

Figure A-1. Trend Analysis of Contractor Personnel by Type of Service Provided in Iraq

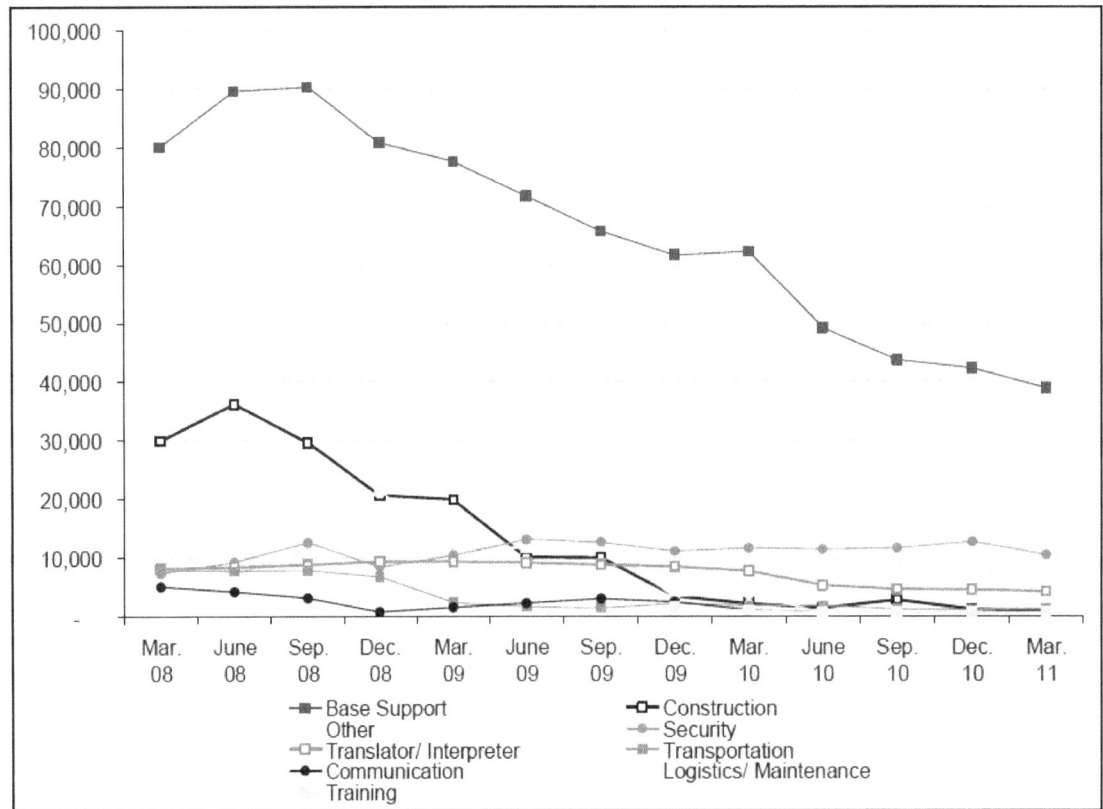

Source: CENTCOM Quarterly Census Reports.

Notes: DOD did not separately track Logistics/Maintenance or Training until the first quarter of 2010. Percentage Breakdown of Contractors in Iraq by Nationality.

Table A-1. Number of Contractor Personnel in Iraq by Type of Service Provided

Date	Base Support	Security	Translator/ Interpreter	Construction	Transport	Training	Communication	Logistics/ Maintenance	Other
Mar. '08	80,150	7,259	8,136	29,937	7,774	--	5,029	--	11,103
June '08	89,716	9,193	8,399	36,224	7,702	--	4,096	--	7,098
Sep. '08	90,386	12,633	8,798	29,626	7,771	--	3,010	--	11,222
Dec. '08	80,931	8,380	9,268	20,729	6,685	--	700	--	21,357
Mar. '09	77,669	10,422	9,241	19,941	2,383	--	1,460	--	11,494
June '09	71,783	13,145	9,128	10,090	1,616	--	2,183	--	11,761
Sep. '09	65,763	12,684	8,765	9,933	1,375	--	2,983	--	12,228
Dec. '09	61,725	11,095	8,414	3,385	2,060	1,458	2,429	6,085	3,384
Mar. '10	62,295	11,610	7,661	2,171	1,796	918	1,004	3,684	4,322
June '10	49,256	11,413	5,165	1,336	1,782	574	603	488	9,004
Sep. '10	43,759	11,628	4,572	2,753	1,115	626	646	445	8,562
Dec. '10	42,386	12,743	4,432	1,144	1,039	591	527	429	7,851
Mar. '11	38,966	10,448	4,099	858	1,229	599	495	324	7,235

Source: CENTCOM Quarterly Census Reports.

Notes: DOD did not separately track logistics/maintenance or training until the first quarter of FY2010.

Appendix B. Contractor and Troop Level Data

The Department of Defense posts the results of its quarterly CENTCOM census report at http://www.acq.osd.mil/log/PS/hot_topics.html. Data is usually posted between six and eight weeks after the end of the quarter. Because the website only posts the most recent two quarters, CRS has provided the data from previous census reports in the tables below.

Table B-1. Contractor Personnel and Troop Level Data for Iraq

Quarter Ending	Total Contractors	U.S. Nationals	Third Country Nationals	Local Nationals	Troop Levels
Sep. 2007	154,825	26,869	45,422	82,534	169,000
Dec. 2007	163,591	31,325	56,368	75,898	165,700
Mar. 2008	149,378	29,351	57,270	62,757	160,500
June 2008	162,428	26,611	62,650	70,167	153,300
Sep. 2008	163,446	28,045	72,109	63,292	146,800
Dec. 2008	148,050	39,262	70,875	37,913	148,500
Mar. 2009	132,610	36,061	60,244	36,305	141,300
June 2009	119,706	31,541	56,125	32,040	134,600
Sep. 2009	113,731	29,944	53,780	30,007	129,200
Dec. 2009	100,035	27,843	51,990	20,202	114,300
Mar. 2010	95,461	24,719	53,549	17,193	95,900
June 2010	79,621	22,761	46,148	10,712	88,320
Sep. 2010	74,106	20,981	42,457	10,668	48,410
Dec. 2010	71,142	19,943	40,776	10,423	47,305
Mar. 2011	64,253	18,393	36,523	9,337	45,660

Source: CENTCOM Quarterly Census Reports and "Boots on the Ground" monthly reports to Congress.

Table B-2. Contractor Personnel and Troop Level Data for Afghanistan

Quarter Ending	Total Contractors	U.S. Nationals	Third Country Nationals	Local Nationals	Troop Levels
Sep. 2007	29,473	3,387	2,864	23,222	24,500
Dec. 2007	36,520	5,153	3,815	27,552	24,600
Mar. 2008	52,336	4,220	4,678	43,438	28,800
June 2008	41,232	4,724	4,121	32,387	34,000
Sep. 2008	68,252	5,405	4,381	58,466	33,500
Dec. 2008	71,755	5,960	5,232	60,563	32,500
Mar. 2009	68,197	9,378	7,043	51,776	52,300
June 2009	72,968	10,036	11,806	51,126	55,100
Sep. 2009	104,101	9,322	16,349	78,430	62,300
Dec. 2009	107,292	10,016	16,551	80,725	69,000
Mar. 2010	112,092	16,081	17,512	78,499	79,100
June 2010	107,479	19,103	14,984	73,392	93,800
Sep. 2010	70,599	20,874	15,503	34,222	96,600
Dec. 2010	87,483	19,381	21,579	46,523	96,900
Mar. 2011	90,339	20,413	23,537	46,389	99,800

Source: CENTCOM Quarterly Census Reports and "Boots on the Ground" monthly reports to Congress.

Appendix C. Comparison of CRS, CBO, and GAO Methodology for Determining DOD Contract Obligations in Afghanistan and Iraq

In 2008, CBO published a report that tracked the U.S. government's obligations in Iraqi theater from FY2005-FY2007 using FPDS-NG data.[83] CRS used the same methodology in determining the value of contract obligations in the Afghanistan and Iraq theaters, relying on the data in federal government's FPDS database to conduct its analysis. Differences in the data reported by CBO in its 2008 report can be attributed to FPDS, which subsequent to the release of the CBO report, has continuously updated information and restated prior years.

For the past three years, GAO published annual reports on contracting in Afghanistan and Iraq.[84] The GAO reports included only information on contracts performed in Iraq and Afghanistan. However, in some cases, these contracts included performance in other countries as well. Because of how DOD reported the data to GAO, GAO could not isolate the portion of obligations that were specific to Afghanistan or Iraq. GAO did not include in its analysis contracts performed wholly outside of Afghanistan and Iraq but still within the respective theaters of operations. GAO's analysis did not rely exclusively on FPDS data: GAO also reviewed manually compiled lists of obligations and deobligations, and took other steps to refine the data.

The data used by CRS and CBO allocates place of performance based on the principal place of performance as indentified by FPDS. Because FPDS only allows for one country to be listed as the place of performance, contracts listed as being performed in one country can also involve substantial performance in other countries. As a result of differences in methodologies, some contract obligations may be allocated to different countries by GAO, CRS, and CBO.

---

[83] Congressional Budget Office, *Contractors' Support of U.S. Operations in Iraq*, August 2008.

[84] U.S. Government Accountability Office, *Contingency Contracting: DOD, State, and USAID Contracts and Contractor Personnel in Iraq and Afghanistan*, 09-19, October 1, 2008. See also U.S. Government Accountability Office, *Contingency Contracting: DOD, State, and USAID Continue to Face Challenges in Tracking Contractor Personnel and Contracts in Iraq and Afghanistan*, 10-1, October 1, 2009. See also U.S. Government Accountability Office, *Iraq and Afghanistan: DOD, State, and USAID Face Continued Challenges in Tracking Contracts, Assistance Instruments, and Associated Personnel*, 11-1, October 1, 2010.

Table C-1. Total Contract Action Obligations for Afghanistan

	FY2005	FY2006	FY2007	FY2008	FY2009	FY2010
Afghanistan	$1,566,743,610	$2,369,796,988	$3,195,878,220	$5,952,398,745	$7,146,505,524	$11,266,769,733
Kazakhstan	$29,696,861	$7,495,471	$5,113,688	$26,038,365	$41,970,867	$59,116,526
Kyrgyzstan	$61,751,645	$32,297,583	$360,291,188	$17,568,564	$326,688,826	$119,507,687
Pakistan	$33,710,475	$162,445,997	$62,848,359	$203,365,810	$221,731,297	$156,860,439
Tajikistan	$495,329	$20,626	$0	$11,000	$951,307	$3,384,903
Turkmenistan	$13,278,462	$17,800,196	($497,308)	$194,688,206	$14,258,634	$180,515,672
Uzbekistan	$48,542,478	($10,210,717)	$11,763,398	$13,910,651	$8,646,691	$20,271,894

Source: FPDS-NG, January 26, 2011, for FY2005-FY2010.

Table C-2. Total Contract Action Obligations for Iraq

	FY2005	FY2006	FY2007	FY2008	FY2009	FY2010
Iraq	$13,936,557,118	$12,880,086,264	$12,424,968,873	$15,140,815,305	$9,204,318,064	$6,918,071,383
Bahrain	$498,830,223	$675,802,906	$496,862,601	$1,124,966,805	$1,913,164,861	$499,866,486
Jordan	$107,941,450	$366,463,184	$70,750,722	$77,883,341	$11,248,812	$12,659,106
Kuwait	$2,159,410,194	$4,556,048,622	$4,159,363,917	$4,159,365,050	$5,076,239,693	$4,475,580,322
Qatar	$186,755,204	$126,924,969	$223,458,228	$333,434,881	$738,243,100	$273,770,839
Saudi Arabia	$770,658,807	$794,222,528	$175,467,136	$316,466,796	$853,899,470	$713,507,658
Turkey	$106,538,349	$256,684,243	$317,177,234	$162,519,116	$273,977,092	$127,228,630
UAE	$399,298,596	$667,304,112	$226,104,619	$1,122,186,089	$293,421,407	$2,368,834,180

Source: FPDS-NG, January 26, 2011, for FY2005-FY2010.

Author Contact Information

Moshe Schwartz
Specialist in Defense Acquisition
mschwartz@crs.loc.gov, 7-1463

Joyprada Swain
Research Associate
jswain@crs.loc.gov, 7-5973